COWFOLK'S GUIDE
TO
GETTING
OLDER

COWFOLK'S GUIDE TO GETTING OLDER

Judge Roy English

GIBBS SMITH
TO ENRICH AND INSPIRE HUMANKIND

Life isn't about how fast you run or how high you climb,

but how well you bounce.

SOME FOLKS HAVE TO SNORE IN SELF-DEFENSE.

It's hard to keep a blanket
on the naked truth.

THE DIFFERENCE IN KNOW-HOW AND WISDOM IS IN THE DOING.

**Don't fry frog legs
in an open skillet.**

Don't envy your sister. The violet is not diminished by the beauty of the rose.

COUNTRY FOLKS CAN MAKE
DO WITH MIGHTY LITTLE.

EVEN STUBBORN MULES KNOW YOU HAVE TO PULL TOGETHER.

WISDOM
IS MOSTLY
LEARNING
HOW TO PACE
YOURSELF.

GOING TO BED MAD IS NO FUN, BUT IT'S BETTER THAN FIGHTING ALL NIGHT.

When mowing a pasture, remember that a bumble bee is faster than a farm tractor.

LIFE ISN'T ALWAYS FAIR, BUT THINGS HAVE A WAY OF WORKING OUT.

Older country folks know a lot of stuff

that ain't wrote down nowhere.

LIFE IS SIMPLER WHEN YOU PLOW AROUND THE STUMPS.

A PERSON MUST MEET FEAR TO KNOW COURAGE.

Don't share a crosscut saw with a quitter.

TROUBLE IS A PRIVATE THING.

DON'T LEND IT, AND DON'T BORROW IT.

IT DOESN'T TAKE
A VERY BIG PERSON TO
CARRY A GRUDGE.

Don't sneeze behind a skittish mule.

DON'T SELL YOUR MULE TO BUY A PLOW. THINK ABOUT IT.

LEARN WHAT'S IMPORTANT AND WHAT'S NOT.

DON'T BLAME THE WORM FOR NOT WANTING TO GO FISHING.

A FANCY TITLE IS ABOUT
AS USEFUL AS THE CURL
IN A PIG'S TAIL.

NO WOMAN IS TRULY FREE UNTIL SHE CAN CHANGE A FLAT TIRE.

Little folks have
big ears and even
bigger eyes.

FORGIVE YOUR ENEMIES. IT MESSES WITH THEIR HEADS.

INTEREST ON DEBT NEVER SLEEPS.

The difference between young liars and old thieves is just a matter of time.

Go bowling! Enjoy a game of poker!
Eat prunes and be a regular guy!

EXPRESS YOURSELF KINDLY.

BEING HONEST DOESN'T MEAN BEING CRUEL.

Forget about justice. Just do what's right.

IT'S BEST TO STOP TALKING ONCE YOU'VE SAID ALL YOU KNOW.

**Refuse to grow
old gracefully, and
leave this world
like you came in—**

**kicking, squalling,
and raising a stink.**

NOTHING IS IMPOSSIBLE

★ ★ ★

EXCEPT PEEING IN A NAKED MAN'S POCKET.

FOLKS WHO EXPECT TO LIVE HAPPILY EVER AFTER HAD BEST TEND TO IT DAILY.

HERE'S TO OLD COOTS AND FREE SPIRITS—LONG MAY THEY DANCE!

Folks don't
change.
They just get
more so.

THE ACORN DOESN'T FALL FAR FROM THE TREE.

BUT SOME NUTS ROLL A LONG WAY FROM THEIR ROOTS.

Lazy and Quarrelsome are ugly sisters.

ALWAYS DANCE WITH THE ONE YOU CAME WITH— UNLESS YOU CAME WITH YOUR COUSIN.

LEARN FROM THE TEAPOT:

WHISTLE WHEN YOU NEED TO LET OFF STEAM.

Don't go hunting
with a fella named
Chug-a-Lug.

BUTTER YOUR PILLS SO THEY DON'T GET HUNG IN YOUR ESOPHAGUS.

WORK HARD TO BE GOOD, NOT PERFECT.

Courtship is dancing in the moonlight; marriage is washing socks.

CARRY DRIED DOG AND CAT
FOOD IN THE BACK OF YOUR
TRUCK FOR OLD STRAYS THAT
YOU COME ACROSS.

FEELING SORRY FOR YOURSELF IS A LONELY RIDE.

A cheerful heart makes
a tough job easier.

Don't rock
back on a
three-legged
stool.

ENVY SICKENS A BODY.

You can earn
contempt in a
heartbeat.

Respect

takes time.

LOOSE TONGUES AND TIGHT BOOTS CAUSE A LOT OF PAIN.

TREES THAT DON'T BEND BREAK IN THE WIND.

Carrying a grudge makes a strong person weak.

Don't corner something that
is meaner than you.

COWFOLKS LAUGH WHEN YOU LAUGH,
CRY WHEN YOU CRY,
KNOW WHEN YOU'RE SICK,
AND CARE WHEN YOU DIE.

Make it your ambition to lead a quiet life and mind your own business.

CREAM RISES
TO THE TOP,
BUT SO DOES
SOME STINKY STUFF.

Whatever the illness,

★ ★ ★

time is the
best cure.

ENTHUSIASM IS THE SAUCE THAT FLAVORS OUR DAYS.

AN OUNCE OF DOING IS WORTH A POUND OF TALK.

Express yourself! In your spare time, show up at public meetings and raise hell about whatever is on the agenda.

WHEN LIFE THROWS YOU FOR A LOOP, ENJOY THE FLIGHT AND THEN GET BACK IN THE SADDLE.

When in doubt, pray on it.

A WHISTLED TUNE IS SOUL MUSIC.

REMEMBER, SOME FOLKS HAVE 20 YEARS OF EXPERIENCE; OTHERS HAVE ONE YEAR OF EXPERIENCE 20 TIMES.

FOR A HAPPY MARRIAGE, VIEW YOUR MATE THROUGH A TELESCOPE, NOT A MICROSCOPE.

Keep talking to your kids, no matter what.

FIGURE OUT WHAT YOU STAND FOR—AND WHAT YOU WON'T.

73

If it ain't broke, chances are it will be.

MOST SHORTCUTS ARE DEAD ENDS.

Every grandparent knows there is greater joy in loving than in being loved.

A WISE MAN IS QUICK TO LISTEN AND SLOW TO SPEAK.

A person who
doesn't stand
for something
★★★
will fall for
anything.

EARLY TO BED AND EARLY
TO RISE WILL PRETTY
MUCH SHUT DOWN THE
DOMINO GAME.

VISIT A HISTORY CLASS AT THE COMMUNITY COLLEGE

AND ARGUE WITH THE TEACHER WHEN SHE GETS IT WRONG.

IT'S NEVER TOO LATE TO PLAN FOR
THE FUTURE, BUT ALSO REMEMBER
WHAT YOU PLANNED FOR TODAY.

FINANCE A FISHING CABIN WITH A 30-YEAR MORTGAGE SO YOUR CHILDREN WILL REMEMBER YOU WHEN YOU'RE GONE.

When your friends go to New England or Colorado for the fall foliage tour, you can avoid the traffic by going to West Texas. You will also avoid the foliage.

FOR A BIT OF MISCHIEF, GROWL AT NERVOUS LITTLE DOGS IN PUBLIC PLACES AND MAKE THEM BARK FRANTICALLY.

Demonstrate your
steady hand to your
grandchildren by
sharing your talent
for eating peas
with a table knife.

BEING NEIGHBORLY
DOESN'T MEAN STICKING
YOUR NOSE IN SOMEBODY
ELSE'S BUSINESS.

BELIEVING IN SOMETHING MAKES IT POSSIBLE, NOT EASY.

LIFE IS A GAME.

THOSE WHO LOVE MOST, WIN.

Your ways teach
more than
your words.

IT'S HARD TO MAKE
SOMEONE SMILE WITHOUT
SMILING YOURSELF.

YOU CAN'T UNSAY A CRUEL THING.

Don't lick a frozen pump handle.

Carry your own trail mix of
salted peanuts, Junior Mints,
candy corn, and Rolaids.

LIVING IN THE PAST IS DANCING WITH A DEAD MAN.

DOING THE LORD'S WORK DOESN'T PAY MUCH, BUT THERE'S A FINE RETIREMENT PLAN.

Hope is the seed stock of happiness.

A fella can tell how happy he is going to be in twenty years

by looking at his father-in-law.

FORGIVE AND FORGET THE BEST YOU CAN.

YOU CAN TELL A LOT ABOUT PEOPLE BY WHAT THEY DON'T HAVE.

EVERY PATH HAS SOME PUDDLES.

On special occasions, wear funny hats and loud ties, flowered underwear and bright yellow suspenders. Break all the silly proper rules and be a kid again.

DON'T ARGUE JUST FOR THE HELL OF IT.

COFFEE IS BEST WHEN IT'S SAUCERED AND BLOWED.

ENGAGE TELEPHONE SOLICITORS
IN ENDLESS CHATTER OF YOUR
AILMENTS UNTIL THEY HANG UP.

The shallower the stream, the louder the babble.

A FELLA WHO KEEPS TELLING YOU HOW HONEST HE IS MAY BE TRYING TO CONVINCE HIMSELF.

Telling someone else's secret
is sneaky and low-down.

THE SELF-RIGHTEOUS MESSENGER SPOILS THE MESSAGE.

If you take the
scenic route,

mind that you
slow down and
enjoy the view.

DON'T WHIZ ON AN ELECTRIC FENCE!

MAN DOES NOT LIVE BY BISCUITS ALONE.

Don't try to hold a barn cat against his will.

A WRINKLED FACE DOESN'T MEAN A WRINKLED HEART.

THANK THE
LORD FOR WHAT
HE GAVE YOU,
WHAT HE TOOK
AWAY, AND ALL
YOU HAVE LEFT.

It's hard to get a handle on a problem when you're sitting on your hands.

WANTS AND NEEDS ARE TWO DIFFERENT THINGS.

People should
live below their
means and above
their values.

MAKE YOURSELF USEFUL.

★★★

IF YOU CAN'T WEAVE A BLANKET, MEND A SOCK.

Don't loan money to a friend.
Give it to him. You'll have a
better chance of being repaid.

A SLOW DANCE WITH THE RIGHT PARTNER IS ONE OF LIFE'S SWEETEST PLEASURES. A SLOW DANCE WITH THE WRONG PARTNER IS A TAD AWKWARD.

IN OLD AGE,
FEW REGRET
THE RISKS
THEY TOOK.

Don't carry tales. It's not helpful.

A STEADY PERSON CHANGES WITHOUT CHANGING.

EVERYBODY IS IGNORANT ABOUT SOMETHING.

Old friends started out as new acquaintances.

WE ARE ALL SPOKES OF THE SAME WHEEL.

COWFOLKS LEARN EARLY THAT
A WISHBONE IS NO SUBSTITUTE
FOR A BACKBONE.

A PRAYER IS A KISS ON AN ANGEL'S CHEEK.

WHAT YOU SHOW A CHILD, SHE SHOWS THE WORLD.

The Good Book is a comfort on any trail.

FORBIDDEN LOVE IS A CACTUS BLOOM.

IF YOU BREAK
WIND IN A PUBLIC
PLACE, FROWN
DISGUSTEDLY
AT THE PERSON
BESIDE YOU.

Don't swat a gnat
with a baseball bat.

THOU SHALT NOT GRUMBLE.

If you would
die for
something, you
have something
to live for.

FORGET WHO'S RIGHT; REMEMBER WHAT'S RIGHT.

A snorer hears
everyone's snoring
but his own.

FEED A COLD. STARVE A FEVER.

SOAK A THORN. AIR A WART.

A HORSE IS ONLY AS GOOD AS THE MAN IN THE SADDLE.

MOST OF THE STUFF FOLKS WORRY ABOUT

NEVER HAPPENS.

Cheap boots
are rarely a
bargain.

FOR RUSTY JOINTS, TRY A LITTLE ELBOW GREASE.

SMALL MINDS AND BIG MOUTHS HAVE A WAY OF HOOKING UP.

GET DOWN ON YOUR KNEES
FROM TIME TO TIME AND TRY
TO SNEAK UP ON OLD DOGS,
GRANDKIDS, MOUNTAIN TROUT,
AND THE GOOD LORD.

Don't mistake kindness for weakness.

HORSE RACES ARE
OFTEN WON BY A NOSE
AND A HEART

DON'T RIDE A NEW PATH AT FULL TROT.

Some folks are like ducks. They seem to glide along easy because you can't see how hard they work below the surface.

Sour grapes make bitter wine.

A WHINY COMPANION MAKES FOR A HARD DAY.

LOVE IS MEDICINE — FOR THE ONE WHO GIVES IT AND FOR THE ONE WHO RECEIVES IT.

A CAT THAT LICKS ITS PAW MAY
JUST BE SCRATCHING ITS TONGUE.

Pray for
goodness,
not things.

BEHOLD THE GIFT OF A BRAND NEW DAY.

Take time to call all politicians
who oppose prayer in school and
give them a good cussing.

When you have to
make a big decision,
sleep on it.

JESUS LOVES YOU.

★★★

DEAL WITH IT.

TAKE LITTLE TRIPS INSIDE YOUR HEAD AND VISIT WITH DEPARTED FRIENDS.

NEVER CUSS WHEN YOU'RE WITH SOMEBODY

WITH SOMEBODY

OR WHEN YOU'RE ALONE.

CARRY A SLEEPING BAG TO DOCTOR APPOINTMENTS. IF THEY MAKE YOU WAIT, TAKE A NAP ON THE FLOOR. CHANCES ARE, THEY WILL GET TO YOU QUICKER.

A heart knows
things a head
never will.

LET ANOTHER MAN PRAISE YE, AND NOT THINE OWN LIPS.

If you would
be loved,

try being
lovable.

TEACH YOUR DOG TO FETCH THE NEIGHBOR'S MORNING NEWSPAPER,

BUT ALWAYS RETURN IT AFTER YOU'VE READ IT.

Criticizing someone
else's work won't
improve your own.

CARRY A BUCKET OF PAINT IN YOUR CAR TO CREATE SENIOR-CITIZENS PARKING SPACES WHEREVER YOU THINK THEY SHOULD BE.

A persuasive person has
more than one vote.

REMEMBER TO SAFETY-PIN YOUR SOCKS TOGETHER WHEN YOU WASH THEM SO THE BLUE ONES AND BLACK ONES DON'T TRY TO MATE.

GET OUT YOUR
OLD SCHOOL
PICTURES AND
TOAST THE
MEMORY OF
YOUR FAVORITE
TEACHERS.

NEVER LAY AN ANGRY HAND ON A KID OR AN ANIMAL. IT'S NOT HELPFUL.

REMEMBER, COW CHIPS NEED TO DRY OUT FOR A SPELL BEFORE YOU TOSS THEM.

STAND UP AT THE SPORTSMEN'S
BANQUET AND ANNOUNCE THAT
THE BEST WAY TO HAVE "DUCKS
UNLIMITED" IS TO STOP SHOOTING
THEIR BUTTS OFF.

For cowfolks, retire is something
you do to a tractor.

When you write
an angry letter,
use a pencil.

MAMAS, DON'T LET YOUR LET YOUR COWBOYS

GROW UP TO BE BABIES!

Believe in miracles and look for them every day.

VISIT YOUR KIN,

BUT THINK TWICE BEFORE YOU MOVE IN WITH THEM.

★★★

MANKIND IS THE ONLY CRITTER THAT FEELS THE NEED TO LABEL THINGS AS FLOWERS OR WEEDS.

The only way to learn with your mouth open is to read aloud.

THE SWEETEST PEACHES
ARE JUST OUT OF REACH.

The only cowfolks who sleep late are in the cemetery.

THE BEST SERMONS ARE LIVED, NOT PREACHED.

DON'T STOP TRYING. IF YOU FALL DOWN SEVEN TIMES AND GET UP SIX, YOU MIGHT AS WELL HAVE STAYED DOWN THE FIRST TIME.

Crooked posts
make
crooked fences.

When all else fails, blame the devil.

FORGIVING YOUR ENEMIES DOESN'T GUARANTEE THEY'LL FORGIVE YOU,

★ ★ ★

BUT IT'S A START.

CUT YOUR LOSSES. KNOW WHEN TO DEBIT CASH AND CREDIT EXPERIENCE.

Don't plant more than you can harvest.

Don't harvest more than you can sell, use, or give away.

HAVING A
10 PERCENT
CHANCE OF
RAIN FOR TEN
DAYS DOESN'T
MEAN THERE'S
A 100 PERCENT
CHANCE OF RAIN.

SOMEONE WHO CLAIMS TO WALK ON WATER IS EITHER A HYPOCRITE OR AN ESKIMO.

TELL THE GRANDKIDS YOUR
COMPUTER IS BROKEN
SO THEY WILL HAVE TO
LISTEN TO YOUR STORIES.

TO HAVE A GOOD NEIGHBOR, BE A GOOD NEIGHBOR.

A 30-minute nap after lunch will aid a worker's digestion, improve his attitude, and increase productivity.

A 60-minute nap will ruin
him for the day.

Cowfolks
understand the
circle of life
better than most.

AGE DOESN'T GUARANTEE WISDOM ANY MORE THAN YOUTH GUARANTEES AMBITION.

COUNTRY RIDDLE:

Unlike most of God's creatures, why is it that mules never leave anything to their kids?

ANSWER:

Mules can't reproduce.

KEEP A CAN OF EARTHWORMS AND
A BUCKET OF MINNOWS IN THE
REFRIGERATOR IN CASE YOU WANT
TO GO FISHING.

A fella who brags about his own humility

will lie about anything.

The bull at the front of the herd has the best view.

ASSESS A TWO-STROKE PENALTY
FOR ANY OLD GOLFING BUDDIES WHO
REQUIRE MEDICAL ATTENTION OR
HAVE TO RELIEVE THEMSELVES IN
THE MIDDLE OF A ROUND.

DON'T WORK FOR AN OUTFIT YOU DON'T BELIEVE IN.

Remember your manners. Promptly return the handkerchief you borrow after you clean your ears and blow your nose.

To forgive an enemy
is easy. To forgive
a friend is hard.

DON'T TELL A ROOSTER HE'S NOT RESPONSIBLE FOR THE SUN COMING UP.

HORSEPOWER IS NO SUBSTITUTE FOR HORSE SENSE.

Experience is a great teacher if it doesn't kill you first.

DON'T WEAR POLYESTER TO A WIENER ROAST.

GOD MADE US WITH TWO EARS AND ONLY ONE TONGUE. THAT SHOULD TELL US SOMETHING.

A ROOSTER THAT CROWS AT MIDNIGHT WON'T MAKE IT PAST SUNDAY.

TWO CAN LIVE AS CHEAPLY AS ONE, ASSUMING ONE DOESN'T EAT.

Debt is a shovel.
It can dig a well
or a grave.

IF YOU CAN HOLD YOUR
TONGUE, YOU WILL HAVE
A BETTER GRIP
ON THE SITUATION.

Around animals and in most other places, a calm demeanor is best.

The difference between fast work and hurried work is know-how.

WE FORGET THE STUFF WE NEED TO REMEMBER

AND REMEMBER THE STUFF WE NEED TO FORGET.

THE COST OF THE WEDDING HAS LITTLE TO DO WITH THE QUALITY OF THE MARRIAGE.

Nobody works
as hard as a
farmer, except
maybe a
farmer's wife.

A FARM DOG KNOWS WHEN TO BARK, WHEN TO BITE, AND WHEN TO STAY UNDER THE PORCH. TAKE A LESSON.

Nothing is quite as silly as an educated fool.

IT TAKES TWO THINGS TO DO A JOB:

TO START AND TO FINISH.

Pride can cripple a healthy person.

COWFOLKS GO
TO SLEEP WITH
THE CHICKENS
SO THEY CAN
WAKE UP WITH
THE ROOSTER.

There's no use
knowing how
to do something
unless you do it.

PICKLES AND PEOPLE ARE SWEET OR SOUR, DEPENDING ON WHETHER THEY WERE SOAKED IN SUGAR OR VINEGAR WHEN THEY WERE LITTLE.

FREELY ADMIT THAT A LOT OF THE TIME, THE YOUNGER GENERATION KNOWS MORE THAN WE DO.

IT'S BETTER TO
DIG A POND IN
A VALLEY THAN
ON A HILLTOP.

RESPECT IS LOVE
IN WORK CLOTHES.

When it comes to telemarketers, the rule you taught the little kids now applies to you: Don't talk to strangers!

THERE'S A SHOVEL TO FIT EVERY HAND. FIND YOURS.

KICKING BACK
ON A CREEK
BANK GIVES A
BODY TIME TO
THINK–OR NOT.

When you lose your temper, you find
stuff you didn't know you had.

A boneheaded
blunder is not
a total loss

if you learn
something from it.

A HEART KNOWS THINGS
A HEAD NEVER WILL.

STUFF TENDS TO BREAK WHEN IT'S LOANED OR BORROWED.

Don't spread your
blanket where a
cat's been digging.

ADMIT YOUR MISTAKES

★ ★ ★

BUT DON'T WALLOW IN THEM.

WHATEVER THE MALADY OF OLD AGE, POSITIVITY IS THE BEST TONIC.

First Edition
23 22 21 20 19   5 4 3 2 1

© 2019 by Roy English

Published by
Gibbs Smith
P.O. Box 667
Layton, Utah 84041

1.800.835.4993 orders
www.gibbs-smith.com

Design by Renee Bond
Printed and bound in China
Gibbs Smith books are printed on either recycled, 100 percent post-consumer
waste, FSC-certified papers or on paper produced from a 100 percent certified
sustainable forest-controlled wood source.

Library of Congress Control Number: 2018951513
ISBN 978-1-4236-5172-7